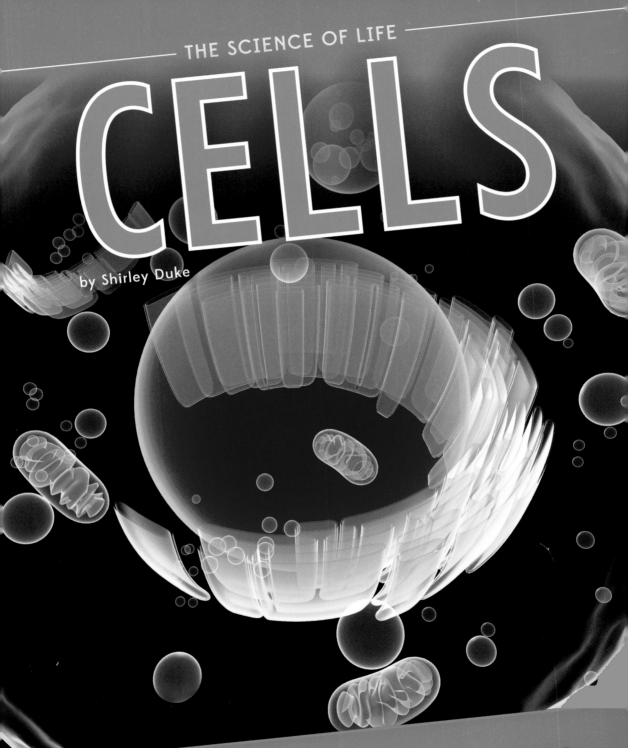

THE SCIENCE OF LIFE

CELLS

by Shirley Duke

Content Consultant
Eric Shelden
Associate Professor
Washington State University

CORE
LIBRARY

Published by ABDO Publishing Company, PO Box 398166, Minneapolis, MN 55439. Copyright © 2014 by Abdo Consulting Group, Inc. International copyrights reserved in all countries. No part of this book may be reproduced in any form without written permission from the publisher. The Core Library™ is a trademark and logo of ABDO Publishing Company.

Printed in the United States of America,
North Mankato, Minnesota
092013
012014

Editor: Arnold Ringstad
Series Designer: Becky Daum

Library of Congress Cataloging-in-Publication Data
Duke, Shirley Smith.
  Cells / by Shirley Duke.
      pages cm -- (The science of life)
  Audience: 8-12.
  Includes index.
  ISBN 978-1-62403-158-8
1. Cells--Juvenile literature. 2. Cytology--Juvenile literature. I. Title.
QH582.5.D85 2014
571.6--dc23
                        2013027634

Photo Credits: Sebastian Kaulitzki/Shutterstock Images, cover, 1; Shutterstock Images, 4, 12, 23, 42 (top), 43; Robert Hooke, 8; Red Line Editorial, 17, 31; PR Courtieu/BSIP/SuperStock, 20; Benjamin Campillo/BSIP/SuperStock, 28; Jacopin/BSIP/SuperStock, 33; Cavallini James/BSIP/SuperStock, 34; MedicalRF/SuperStock, 36; Science Photo Library/SuperStock, 39; Oguz Aral/Shutterstock Images, 42 (bottom)

CONTENTS

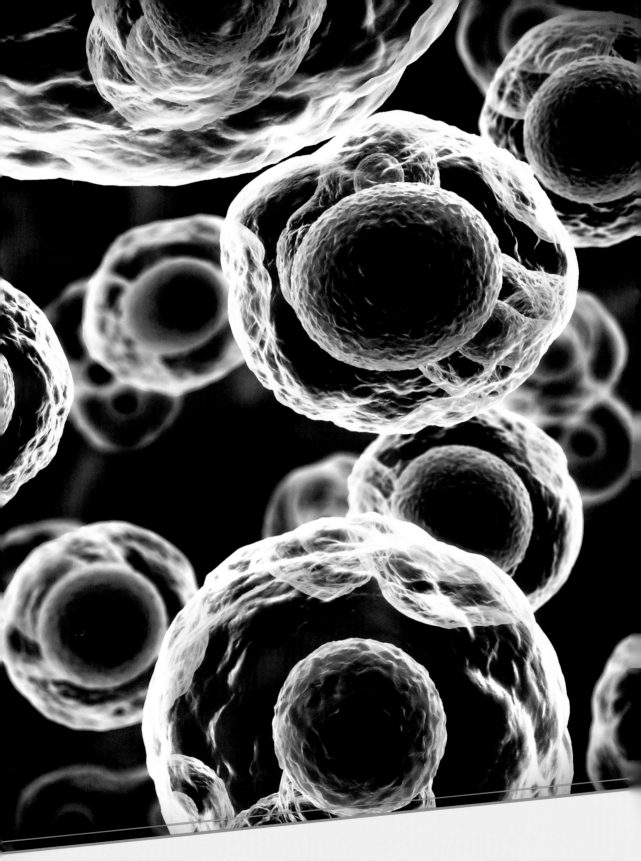

CHAPTER ONE

DISCOVERING CELLS

Cells make you into the person you are. They control the way you look and the way your body works. Everything from your height to your eye color comes from cells and the stuff inside them. They turn the food you eat into energy and help you remember your phone number. Most cells are so tiny you can't even see them. But there are huge numbers of them all around us. Cells are the building

Every living thing is made of cells, from you to elephants to turnips.

blocks of all living things. Each human being is made up of about 100 trillion cells.

Cells are held together by cell membranes or cell walls. These are barriers that hold all the parts of the cell inside. Membranes also make up the boundaries of structures within cells. These structures are called organelles. Just as humans have organs, such as kidneys and lungs, cells have organelles. Like human organs, organelles have special jobs to do. Together, organelles help their cell do its job. Different cells in the body have different jobs. Cells in the heart help pump blood through your body. Cells in the bones help keep your body steady. One organelle, known as the nucleus, acts like a brain for the cell. It tells everything else in the cell what to do.

Some organisms are made of only one cell. Bacteria are one example of this. Bacteria inside your body help process food. Other organisms are multicellular, meaning they contain many cells. Plants and animals, including you, fall into this category.

They are large groups of cells working together to do complicated activities. For example, playing a game of chess takes many cells. Your eye cells see where the pieces are. Your brain cells think of a move. And your muscle cells move your hand.

Seeing Cells

The tiny size of cells means that they were invisible for most of human history. Before scientists could study cells, they had to invent a way to see them. A Dutch scientist created an early microscope in the 1590s. It had more than one lens. Having two lenses gave a clearer and closer view of tiny objects. However, cells were still not visible using this early microscope. English scientist Robert Hooke

Naming Cells

Besides being a skilled inventor and scientist, Robert Hooke came up with the term *cells*. When looking at cork under a microscope, he was reminded of the small rooms in a monastery where priests lived. These rooms were known as cells. The word *cell* originally comes from a Latin word meaning "small compartment."

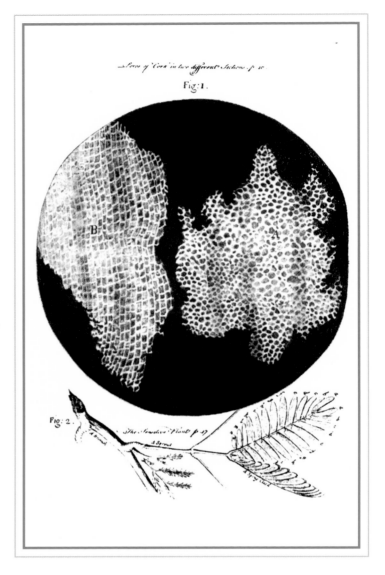

Hooke included a sketch of the cork he saw under the microscope in his book *Micrographia*.

discovered and named cells while looking at a piece of cork under an improved microscope in 1663.

Later in the 1600s, Dutch scientist Antonie van Leeuwenhoek made his own microscopes to study cells. He looked at both plant and animal cells. He was the first to see microorganisms swimming in water. Microorganisms are living things that can only be seen with the help of a microscope. Leeuwenhoek called them *animalcules*, meaning "little animals." Along with living things, he also looked at fossils and crystals under his microscopes.

Cell Theory

A big breakthrough in the study of cells came in 1838. In that year, German scientists Theodor Schwann and Matthias Schleiden met to discuss their ideas about cells. Schleiden had studied cells in plants. Schwann had studied them in animals. Together, they developed a new idea

Lenses and Light

Antonie van Leeuwenhoek was good at taking chunks of glass and grinding them into smooth lenses for his microscopes. These high-quality lenses made objects appear more clearly. Leeuwenhoek's microscopes also used light to give a better view of objects. Modern microscopes still use light. The best modern microscopes make it possible to clearly see single cells and even the organelles inside them.

that later grew into modern cell theory. Cell theory has three parts. First, it says all living things are made of cells. Second, it says that cells are the basic building blocks of these living things. Finally, it says that cells make new cells by dividing in two. These ideas revolutionized biology, the branch of science that involves the study of living things.

It took scientists and inventors centuries of work to develop the microscope and cell theory. Once these technologies and ideas were in place, scientists kept working to build on their knowledge. Amazing discoveries were made over the next few hundred years. Even today, new facts are still being learned about how cells work to make you who you are.

Robert Hooke wrote long descriptions of his observations. In this passage from his book *Micrographia*, he describes looking at cork under his microscope:

> *I Took a good clear piece of Cork, and with a Pen-knife sharpen'd as Keen as a Razor, I cut a piece of it off . . . examining it diligently with a Microscope, me thought I could perceive it to appear a little porous; but I could not so plainly distinguish them, as to be sure that they were pores . . . I with the same sharp Pen-knife, cut off from the former smooth surface an exceeding thin piece of it, and placing it [under the microscope] . . . and casting the light on it . . . I could exceeding plainly perceive it to be all perforated and porous, much like a Honey-comb, but that the pores of it were not regular.*
>
> Source: Robert Hooke. Micrographia. *Royal Society, 1667. Project Gutenberg. Web. Accessed May 17, 2013.*

Nice View

After reading Hooke's description and looking at his sketch in this chapter, write your own description of the cork in modern language. Imagine you are looking under the microscope yourself. How would you describe what you see? If you had discovered them, what would you have called the tiny compartments?

CHAPTER TWO

WHAT'S IN A CELL?

The job of cells is to keep living things alive. Their organelles make it possible for them to do this important job. By working together, the organelles help keep everything from trees to dogs to bacteria to you alive. But the organelles would be useless if they drifted apart. Cells must be able to hold all of their parts inside.

The cell's many parts have different sizes, shapes, and functions.

In animal cells, a cell membrane does two things for the cell. First, it holds the cell together. Second, it lets only certain things, such as water and nutrients, into the cell. Plant cells have cell walls in addition to cell membranes. The walls are stiffer than cell membranes. They let plant cells hold lots of water without bursting. Both animal and plant cells are filled with a jelly-like substance called cytoplasm. Cytoplasm takes up space and holds organelles in place.

The Organelles

One important organelle is the nucleus. It acts like the brain of the cell and tells the other parts what to do. The nucleus holds a special chemical called deoxyribonucleic acid (DNA). The DNA contains a set of instructions telling which proteins are needed to make the entire plant or animal. Many structures in the body, including muscles and hair, are made of proteins. Proteins also help in the body's chemical reactions and in its defense against infections.

The nucleus works closely with other organelles called ribosomes. Ribosomes build proteins. They receive instructions from the DNA about which proteins to make. The proteins are either used by the cell itself, or they are sent out to different cells in the body. Proteins are used to build body structures, such as muscle. Some ribosomes float free in the cytoplasm. Others hook on to an organelle called the endoplasmic reticulum (ER). The ER is a connected group of membranes. It helps move materials, such as proteins, around the cell.

Mitochondria are organelles that turn sugar into energy. Cells use

The ER

There are two kinds of ER. Each has a different job. Smooth ER looks like a group of flat tubes. It stores materials that the cell may need soon. Rough ER is covered in ribosomes. This gives it a bumpy appearance. Its job is to store the proteins created by its ribosomes. When a protein is made, the rough ER creates a bubble around it and moves it to where it is needed.

this energy to do their many jobs, such as creating proteins. Cells that need lots of energy have more mitochondria. If a cell isn't getting enough energy, its mitochondria can split in two to create even more energy. Mitochondria are found in both plant and animal cells.

Both animal and plant cells also contain organelles called vacuoles. These are membranes used to hold water, waste, and other materials. Animal cells often have several small vacuoles. Plant cells usually contain one huge vacuole that can take up 80 percent of the cell. Plant cells use their vacuoles mainly to store water. The water puts pressure on the strong cell wall. This pressure is what makes plant tissue rigid.

Another organelle found in both plant and animal cells is the lysosome. These are like the stomachs of the cell. They break down the cell's waste and worn-out parts. Afterwards, the cell can reuse some of the leftover materials.

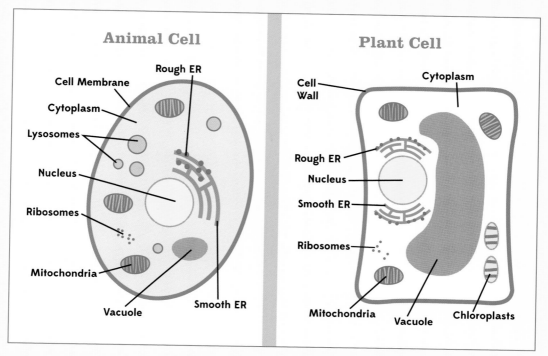

Animal Cells versus Plant Cells

Take a look at these pictures of plant and animal cells. Two major differences are that plant cells have cell walls and chloroplasts, while animal cells do not. Why do you think plants have these parts and animals don't?

However, some organelles are not found in both plant and animal cells. Plant cells have special organelles called chloroplasts. The chloroplasts contain a material called chlorophyll. Chlorophyll is what gives green plants their color. The chloroplasts make it possible for plants to create their own food. They use light, water, and carbon dioxide gas to

Plant Food

After photosynthesis, plants either use or store the energy they create. The energy is stored in many places within plants. Roots, stems, leaves, and fruit are all used to hold this energy. Apples, potatoes, and berries are just a few of the many foods we eat that contain plants' energy.

make sugar and oxygen. This process is called photosynthesis. The sugar created during photosynthesis can later be used by the cell's mitochondria to produce energy.

Theodor Schwann helped create cell theory. He wrote about his meetings with Matthias Schleiden, who worked with him on the theory. Here, he describes the moment he realized how important cell theory could be to biology:

> *One day when I was dining with M. Schleiden, this illustrious botanist pointed out to me the role that the nucleus plays in the development of plant cells. I at once recalled having seen a similar organ in the cells of the notochord [backbone], and in the same instant I grasped the extreme importance that my discovery would have if I succeeded in showing that this nucleus plays the same roles in the cells of the notochord as does the nucleus of plants in the developing plant cells.*
>
> Source: Frederick L. Holmes, Jurgen Renn, and Hans-Jörg Rheinburger. *Reworking the Bench: Research Notebooks in the History of Science. Boston: Kluwer, 2003. Print. 130.*

What's the Big Idea?

In this passage, Theodor Schwann writes about the moment he realized a new discovery. Write a paragraph explaining what he discovered about the relationship between plant and animal cells. Include evidence for why his discovery is important.

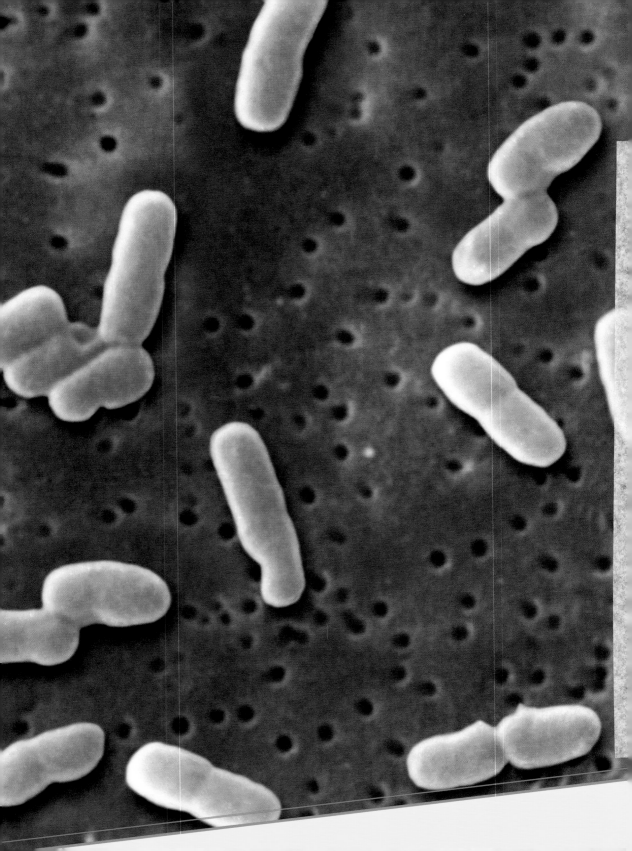

CHAPTER THREE

KINDS OF CELLS

The two basic types of cells are eukaryotic and prokaryotic. In eukaryotic cells, a membrane surrounds the nucleus and holds the cell's DNA. Prokaryotic cells don't have this membrane. Their DNA floats freely in the cytoplasm. Most prokaryotic organisms are made of just one cell. On the other hand, many eukaryotic organisms are made

Prokaryotic organisms are among the smallest and simplest living things.

of many cells working together. All plant and animal cells are eukaryotic.

Animals are made up of three main kinds of cells. The first are somatic cells, also called body cells. They make up most parts of the body. The second are gametes. These are the cells that make reproduction possible. The third are stem cells. They are special cells that can turn into many other kinds of cells. Scientists believe stem cells may someday be used to heal people and cure diseases. Together, the three kinds of cells make it possible for animals to live and reproduce.

Body Cells

Most cells in animals are body cells. They make up the skin, muscles, and organs. When more body cells are needed, a cell divides to form two new cells. Before this division happens, a cell copies its DNA so that it has two complete sets. This lets each of the two new cells have a full DNA set.

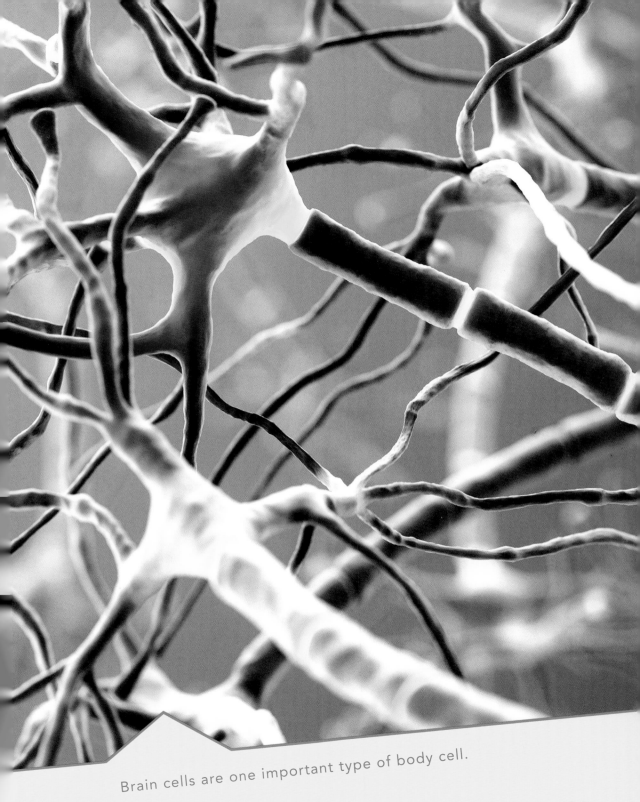

Brain cells are one important type of body cell.

Some cells live for a long time. Nerve cells often live for their owner's entire lifetime. However, cells in many parts of the body are constantly being damaged or destroyed. For example, skin cells can have a lifetime of just a few weeks. Some blood cells live only a few hours! This means it is important for new body cells to be made all the time.

Largest and Smallest

The largest and smallest human cells are both gametes. The female gamete, called the ovum, is the largest at about 0.004 inches (0.1 mm) wide. The male gamete, known as the sperm cell, is the smallest human cell. About 40 times smaller than the ovum, it measures just 0.0001 inches (0.0025 mm) wide.

Gametes

Gametes are the cells that make it possible for animals to reproduce. Each gamete contains one copy of the animal's DNA. When two animals mate, a gamete from one joins with a gamete from the other. The combined cell soon begins to divide over and over again.

The dividing cells eventually grow into a baby animal. The animal gets half of its DNA from its father and half from its mother. The combination means that the new animal has some things in common with one parent and some things in common with the other.

Stem Cells

Stem cells are able to grow into other kinds of cells. When young animals are developing, their stem cells turn into all the kinds of cells needed to create their growing bodies. These developing animals are called embryos. Their stem cells are known as embryonic stem cells. Stem cells can turn into the cells that form the heart, skin, nerves,

Adult Stem Cells

Stem cells are not just found in young animals. Adult stem cells are found in bones, gums, and blood. An adult stem cell does not turn into a particular kind of cell until it is needed. It can form cells like the tissue it came from. However, adult stem cells cannot turn into as many kinds of cells as embryonic stem cells.

and other parts. They can become somatic cells or gametes. Today, scientists are doing research with stem cells. Since these cells can turn into cells from many different body parts, they may help people heal when parts of their bodies are diseased or injured.

Plant Cells

Plants also have body cells, gametes, and stem cells. However, plant cells are divided into other groups based on what they do.

Parenchyma cells are the most common. They do many different jobs within plant cells. These cells are used as storage in fruits and roots. They repair the plant if it is damaged. They are also where photosynthesis takes place.

Collenchyma and sclerenchyma cells are used for support in stems and leaves. They help hold the plant upright. Tracheid cells and vessel elements are also used for support, but they have another function too. They transport water and minerals throughout the plant. Sieve tube members and companion cells are also used for transport. They move food to wherever the plant needs it.

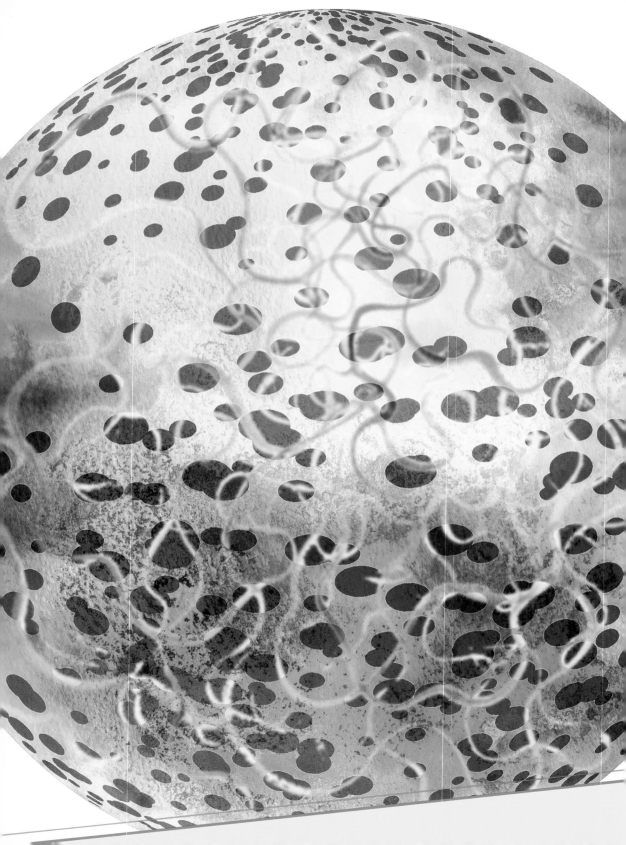

CHAPTER FOUR

CONTROL CENTER

The nucleus is the largest part of most eukaryotic cells. It is surrounded by a membrane called the nuclear envelope. The nuclear envelope holds the cell's DNA. It acts much like the cell membrane, allowing materials to move in and out of the nucleus.

The nucleus is packed with DNA.

DNA and RNA

Inside the nucleus, the cell's DNA exists in long strands. These strands look like ladders twisted into spirals. This shape is called a double helix. The sides of the ladder are made of sugars and chemicals called phosphates. Each rung of the ladder is made of a pair of chemicals known as bases. There are four possible bases in DNA. The order of bases along the strand makes up genetic code.

The genetic code tells the ribosomes what combination of proteins to build. Some combinations of proteins will make a person tall. Others will give a person red hair or green eyes. Some protein combinations even make it more likely for a person

Proteins

Proteins have many jobs within the human body. Some are enzymes, which speed up chemical reactions. The protein keratin helps make skin, hair, and nails. The protein elastin is in skin and blood vessels. Proteins are built out of chemicals called amino acids. Different combinations of amino acids make up different proteins.

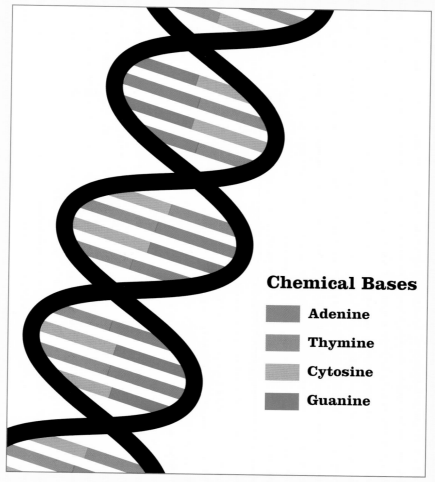

Chemical Bases

Adenine

Thymine

Cytosine

Guanine

DNA Structure

This illustration shows the double helix DNA structure. Each base is shown in a different color. Do you notice anything about how the bases are arranged? Do certain bases seem to go together?

to get a certain disease. Each piece of the genetic code that has instructions for making a specific protein is called a gene.

The DNA is in the nucleus, but the ribosomes that make proteins are outside the nucleus. How do the instructions get out to the ribosomes? Another chemical called ribonucleic acid (RNA) copies genetic code and takes it from the nucleus to the ribosomes. When it's time to make protein, a section of DNA splits in half between the bases. A protein called RNA polymerase attaches to one of the sides and copies the DNA code into RNA. Then, the RNA leaves the nucleus through the nuclear membrane. It travels to the ribosomes and delivers the instructions for making proteins.

Chromosomes

Inside the nucleus, the DNA is organized into structures called chromosomes. Different organisms can have differing numbers of chromosomes. People have 23 pairs of chromosomes, totaling 46 in all. Twenty-two of the pairs look identical in most healthy people. But the twenty-third pair looks different in males and females. They are known as the sex

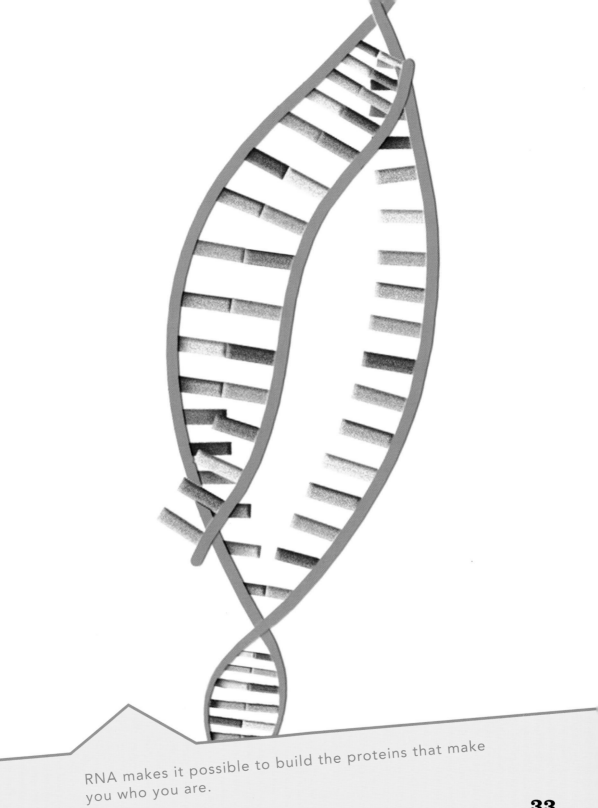

RNA makes it possible to build the proteins that make
you who you are.

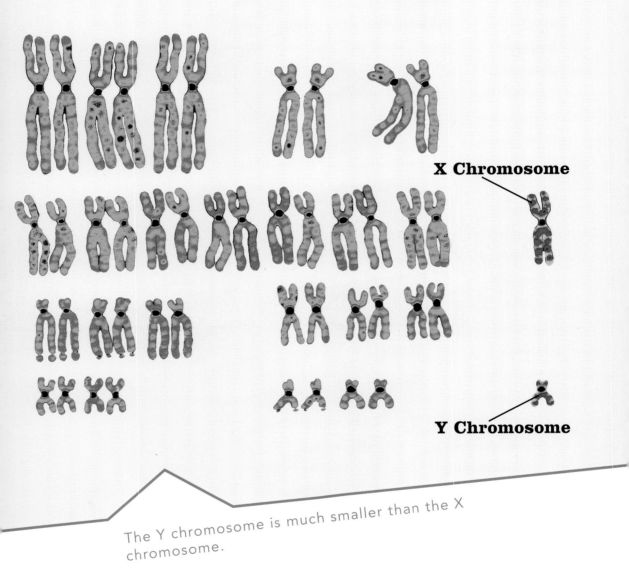

X Chromosome

Y Chromosome

The Y chromosome is much smaller than the X chromosome.

chromosomes. They are named for the letters they look like. Women have two X chromosomes. Men have one X chromosome and one Y chromosome.

About 99 percent of DNA is the same in all people. The last 1 percent is what makes you the person you are. Other than identical twins, every person has a unique set of DNA. Your combination of genes is different from anyone else's.

Chromosome Counts

Organisms with many chromosomes aren't always more complex. Humans have 46 chromosomes, but goldfish have 94. One type of fern has more than 1,000 chromosomes!

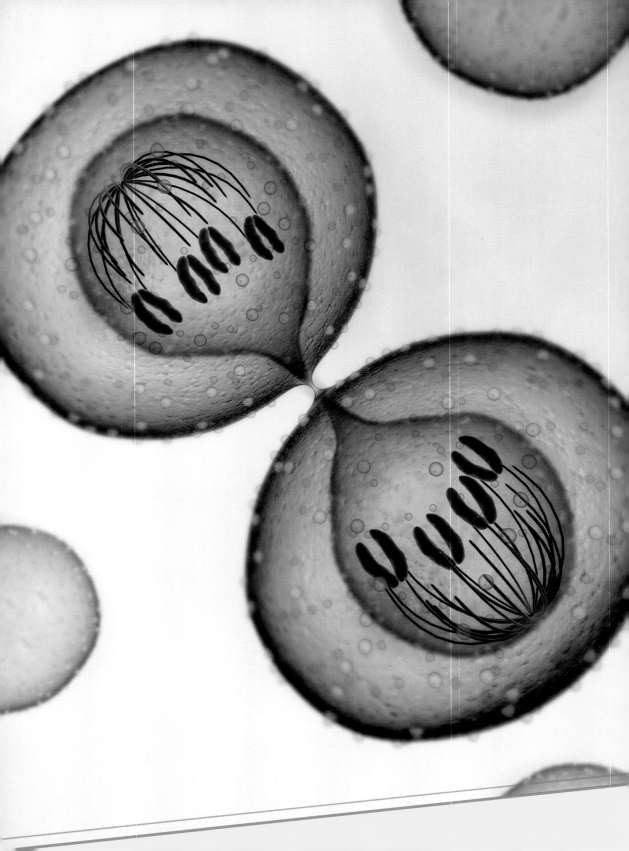

CHAPTER FIVE

MAKING MORE CELLS

One of the key parts of cell theory says that cells divide to make more cells. There are two ways cells divide. Most use a process called mitosis. In mitosis, one cell splits into two identical copies of itself. The original cell is the mother cell, and the copies are the daughter cells. Another kind of division is meiosis. It is used to create gamete cells.

Cell division keeps you healthy and helps you grow.

Mitosis

Mitosis includes four key phases, or steps. Before and after mitosis, cells are in a phase known as interphase. Cells spend most of their time in this phase. Near the end of interphase, cells get ready to divide by copying their DNA into two identical sets of chromosomes. The cell also checks to make sure the DNA isn't harmed or copied incorrectly. The cell can repair problems if it finds them. This helps keep the cell from making failed copies.

Prophase is the first step of mitosis. Inside the nucleus, the DNA thickens and forms tightly packed chromosomes. Then the nuclear envelope dissolves.

Next, in metaphase, the chromosomes line up at the center of the cell. They organize themselves so that each daughter cell will get a complete set of chromosomes. In anaphase, the two sets of chromosomes separate. Each moves to one side of the cell. Finally, in telophase, a new nuclear

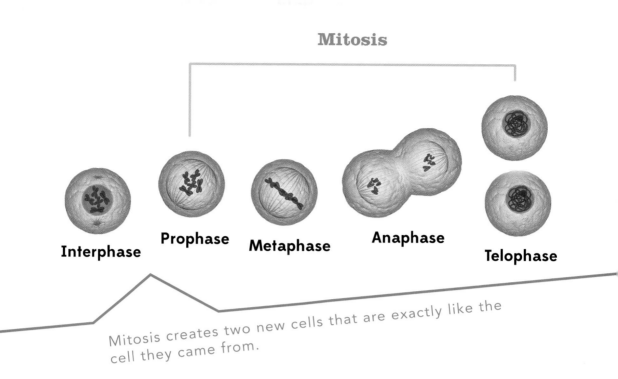

Mitosis

Interphase **Prophase** **Metaphase** **Anaphase** **Telophase**

Mitosis creates two new cells that are exactly like the cell they came from.

envelope forms around each set of chromosomes. The cytoplasm splits apart, creating two separate cells.

Meiosis

A different type of cell division is used to create gamete cells, which are used in reproduction. The process is called meiosis. Meiosis includes the same basic steps as mitosis. Each step is performed twice, but the cell's DNA is only copied once. The end result is four gametes, each with half as many chromosomes as the mother cell. For example, human gametes have 23 single chromosomes. When they join with an

Making Copies

Some organisms can reproduce without gametes. Single-celled bacteria split into two cells that are exactly alike. This process is called fission. Other organisms create their young by growing them from their body. They break off from the parent when grown. They are exact copies of the adult that formed them. This process is called budding. Sponges and jellyfish are animals that can bud their young.

opposite-sex gamete, the combined cell will have a full set of 23 pairs, or 46 total chromosomes.

Cell division is going on inside your body twenty-four hours a day. The new cells and their organelles work together to carry out many tasks. Your DNA and RNA are hard at work copying genetic code. Your mitochondria are creating energy for your muscles to use. Your cell membranes are keeping your cells together. And your ribosomes are building important proteins. Together, your cells and their many parts are always making you who you are.

Using Animation

Cell biologist Janet Iwasa uses animation to show the cell at work. She even went to Pixar, the studio that created such films as *Toy Story* and *Brave*, to learn how to put action in motion. She uses animation to help show the difference between sick cells and healthy ones. She also uses 3D motion to show the way things move into and out of cells. Her work brings cell biology to life for the public. She thinks animation can change the way we think about biology.

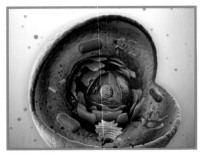

Using 3D graphics makes it easier for students and scientists alike to understand cell processes.

Learning about Hearing

Scientists Richard Rabbitt and William Brownell are studying hair cells in the inner ear. They want to know how these cells help people hear soft sounds better. They found that the hair cells make the motion from sound waves stronger. This happens before the sound waves are picked up by nerve cells. Once the hair cells make the sound waves stronger, the nerves pick up the sound waves and send signals to the brain. The actions of the cells let the brain control how much louder the sound becomes.

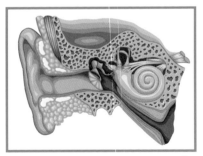

Understanding the cells of the inner ear could make it possible to improve people's hearing.

Stem cell research may unlock exciting new cures for diseases and repairs for injuries.

Stem Cells

Scientists have found a certain protein that can turn stem cells found inside bones into brain cells. These bone cells usually form white blood cells, which fight off infections. But scientist Richard Lerner found that when a certain protein is put into stem cells, they start to form a basic kind of nerve cell. This discovery holds hope for repairing spine and brain injuries.

You Are There

The primary sources included in Chapter One and Chapter Two show the writings of early scientists after they looked at cells under microscopes. Imagine you are one of these early scientists. Think about something you might be interested in looking at under a microscope for the first time. Write a few sentences about what you would look at and what you would expect to find.

Tell the Tale

Chapter Five discusses the process of cell division. Consider the process of mitosis as if you were able to be inside the nucleus as the cell division begins. Follow the stages that you would see taking place. Write a description of your view of the complete process.

Why Do I Care?

Chapter Four discusses how your genetic code gives you a unique set of traits. Chapter Five discusses how mothers and fathers each give one set of chromosomes to their children. What traits do you share with your parents or other relatives?

Another View

Some people oppose using stem cells for research. Have an adult or librarian help you find two sources that discuss the pros and cons of stem cell research. What arguments do the two sources make about being for or against this kind of research? Do they provide additional details about the use of these cells?

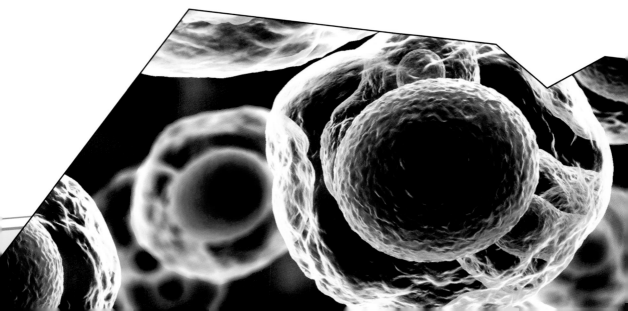

GLOSSARY

biology
the study of life

chromosomes
the parts inside a cell that
carry genetic code

cytoplasm
a jelly-like substance which
fills the space between
organelles in a cell

eukaryotes
cells with a membrane called
an envelope surrounding the
nucleus

membrane
a structure in a living thing
that acts as a barrier or
container

organelles
the organ-like parts that run a
cell's activities

organism
a living thing

prokaryotes
cells that lack a membrane
surrounding their DNA

traits
characteristics of living things

LEARN MORE

Books

Dowdy, Penny. *Animal Cells.* New York: Crabtree, 2010.

Green, Dan. *Human Body: A Book With Guts.* New York: Kingfisher, 2011.

Walker, Richard. *Human Body.* New York: DK, 2009.

Web Links

To learn more about cells, visit ABDO Publishing Company online at **www.abdopublishing.com**. Web sites about cells are featured on our Book Links page. These links are routinely monitored and updated to provide the most current information available.
Visit **www.mycorelibrary.com** for free additional tools for teachers and students.

INDEX

ABOUT THE AUTHOR

Shirley Duke is the author of many science books. She taught science for a number of years and then began to write for young people. Shirley enjoys reading and hiking. She divides her time between Texas and the Jemez Mountains of New Mexico.